RAINBOW OBSIDIAN

RAINBOW OBSIDIAN

PHILLIPS KLOSS

Sunstone Press

Santa Fe, New Mexico

Printed in the United States of America

Library of Congress Cataloging in Publication Data:

Kloss, Phillips Wray, 1902-
    Rainbow Obsidian.

    I. Title.
PS3521.L65R39   1985   811'.52   85-2628
ISBN: 978-0-86534-070-1 (Hardcover) ISBN: 978-1-63293-152-8 (Softcover)

Published in 1985 by Sunstone Press
                Post Office Box 2321
                Santa Fe, NM 87504-2321 / USA

CONTENTS

RAINBOW OBSIDIAN

ENTITY AND IDENTITY

"Where do you come from, baby dear,
Out of the nowhere into the here?"
And see the shapes existing around
And name each one with a different sound
Giving linguistic identity
To every apparent entity.
Thing after thing, fact after fact,
Sensations, perceptions, conceptions intact,
Connections by which you live and act —
Verbality.

And where will you go to, tired old man,
At the end of life's weary articulate span
Loaded with name after name after name
Into the thenceness whence you came,
Sightless and soundless and quite unaware
Of any communicable language there,
Nothing averred,
Not even the word
Eternity.

ABIOGENESIS

We do not know and never will know the origin of life and
    origin of man, whether a slow evolution from single-
    celled organisms to many-celled plants, animals,
    anthropoid apes,
Or a sudden multiplicity of species, spontaneous generation
    of photosynthetic protoplasm, a chemical abiogenesis.
Whatever the forces and sources, whatever the reproductions
    and recapitulations in seed and embryo, the miracle of
    life is a mystery no religion or science will ever solve,
And those of us who love and respect the wondrousness of
    life reject the ridiculous myths about it.
The Adam and Eve myth, the Egyptian, Greek, Roman god-
    myths, the modern ethnological theories are all verbal
    fantasies.
That the so-called American Indians originated in Mongolia
    and emigrated into the so-called New World over a land
    bridge across the Bering Strait is a preposterous
    postulation.
There were ice bridges on both sides of the continent, there
    were comings and goings of unknown peoples prior to
    the Cro-Magnons, our Eskimos still roam half way
    around the Arctic Circle.
Which is not to deny there was a two-way Mongolian traffic,
    but our "indigenous" American Indians largely lack
    Blood Group B, whereas the Mongolians are
    distinguished by Blood Group B.
Various civilizations have risen and perished without a trace,
    strange bones, strange instruments found in the Nevada
    desert indicate a strange species of Homo sapiens
    existed there.

Eight-foot skeletons found in Oklahoma indicate a giant race,
the Negroid features of Olmec sculpture indicate what-
ever you wish to imagine.

Our classification of Proterozoic, Paleozoic, Mesozoic,
Cenozoic, Psychozoic eras will be obliterated in a total
migmatitization of matter.

Temples, churches, mosques, cathedrals, idols, laboratories,
skyscrapers, airplanes, automobiles will be mashed
together with petrified dinosaur bones.

The sun itself is a nuclear explosion constantly regenerating
the energy it emits by reciprocal input from output.

New forms of life will arise from a new abiogenesis, but
the miracle of man's brief existence will remain a
miracle forever in the timelessness of time.

THE ABORIGINAL UTE

The root people, root language of the Southwest on down to
    the Nahuatl Aztecs of Mexico,
Progenitors of the Pithouse, Cliffdweller, Pueblo peoples, of
    the Paiute, Pima, Papago,
Of the fierce Comanche and Kiowa tribes, of the passive
    Shoshonean California tribes,
Ute the root, aboriginal only in the sense of pristine
    habitation, their centrifugal source unknowable.
They expanded and diversified, the Pueblo Indians attaining
    the zenith culture of the so-called Uto-Aztecan linguistic
    stock,
A relatively free independent self-sufficient people,
    individually and socially superior to Toltec, Maya, and
    Inca peoples.
They had no omnipotent priest, king, or emperor demanding
    servitude, no silly adulterous Greek gods meddling in
    their affairs.
They worked with the forces of nature, benign forces, sun
    rain earth, and their head men had to work like every-
    body else,
Raised their own corn, beans, squash, hunted their own meat,
    made their own moccasins and attire, and the women
    wove fiber garments.
It was an egalitarian agrarian society unique in the history of
    the peoples of the world,
And it is a parable against the power-grabbers of modern
    civilization whether communist or capitalist.
Their superstitions and taboos were no worse than the
    credulities and phobias of today.

They were friendly to other people, welcomed a group of
  Keresan-speaking Sioux people into their midst,
And the Keresans adopted their way of life, built sturdy
  pueblos, emulated their ceremonial dances, superlative
  dances still vital at Cochití, Santo Domingo, San Felipe,
  Santa Ana, Zia.
The Mongolian Apache-Navaho hordes were the enemies of
  all Pueblos, they swept down from the north, stole
  Pueblo crops, stole Pueblo women, stole Pueblo land.
The entire Navaho Reservation really belongs to Ute-stock
  peoples, the entire Jicarilla Apache Reservation really
  belongs to Ute-stock peoples.
The Apache-Navahos are not Indians, they have no native
  claim to the gas wells, coal mines, uranium deposits
  developed in that country, they have devastated that
  country with their miserable herds of sheep, goats,
  horses, and lately their ubiquitous pickups.
Granted the esthetic quality of their weaving and sand-
  painting, the Navaho Trail of Beauty is a Trail of Booty,
  their acquisitiveness is intolerable, they must be
  restricted.
Our big-city civilization, the multiple masses of people,
  devastates the country worse than the Navahos, destroys
  the natural beauty of the land, destroys the natural
  resources everywhere, eventually will destroy livability.
We will have to come back to the self-restricting self-
  sufficient precedent the Utean Pueblos set for us, reduce
  our excesses for a freer pursuit of knowledge, pro-
  founder enterprise, rejoice in being alive, sing to
  the sunrise.

PIRO AND PAIUTE

The Piro Indians had the highest culture, the Paiutes the
    lowest in the Ute phylum.
The Piro province extended along the Rio Grande and
    adjacent mountains and plains from what is now El Paso
    to what is now Bernalillo,
Thriving independent pueblos connected by language alone,
    the musical Tiwa tongue, said to be the most archaic
    Indian language, vestigial perhaps from the language
    spoken by the aboriginal Utes.
The Paiutes speak a modern Ute dialect. They were called
    Digger Indians because they lived in the desert and dug
    for edible roots, bulbs, ant eggs, beetles.
They also ate snakes, lizards, lice, mice, rodents, rabbits,
    birds, they wore rabbitskins thonged together, lived in
    brush shelters or burrows, never washed, they were
    filthy, they stank.
The Piros were immaculate. Spanish chroniclers noted their
    cleanliness and friendliness. They wove white cotton
    garments, made excellent pottery, they sang, they
    aspired.
Conversely a rare old photograph of a Paiute maiden, taken
    in the 1860's, shows refined beautiful features,
    intelligent eyes looking straight at you, a haunting face.
She was dressed in dirty rabbitskins but you felt her
    potentialities were unlimited, her adjustment to her
    desert environment greater than a Piro maiden's to hers.

INDIAN PANTHEISM

Red ants were a people to some Pueblo Indians, the activity
    around the granular heap a tribal analogy.
Rattlesnakes were a people too, a different analogy, the
    spread of the Plumed Serpent concept in the Uto-
    Aztecan phylum.
Pantheistically they claimed kinship with every living
    creature from timid creeping mouse to bold soaring
    eagle.
In fact eagles were trapped, confined in wicker cages, their
    tailfeathers pulled out while still alive so that the live
    spirit of the eagles could be attached to headdresses,
    warbonnets, armwhorls.
The Taos Deer Dance is a prayer of thanksgiving to the
    spirits of the deer the Indians killed for meat.
Men dressed in antlered deerhides, representing the slain
    deer, kneel in a circle while two women dressed in
    white robes, representing the Mother Deer, dance
    around the circle.
And they shake a gourd rattle over each antlered head,
    thereby sprinkling a blessing on the spirits of the dead
    deer, a poetic conceit,
But it doesn't alleviate the agony the deer suffered with an
    arrow stuck in their throat or vital organs,
Nor can we reconcile our pity and compassion with the
    brutality of existence.

THE ANTHROPOCENTRIC ATTITUDE

The Greek gods were devised in human shape to expedite
    human affairs and meddle with human fate.
The early church authorities devised an anthropocentric God
    likewise, man was the center of attention, other animals
    had no soul,
Hence it didn't matter how badly they were abused, horses
    were whipped so hard they died in the harness.
Spanish and Mexican people make a sport of baiting a bull
    in a bullring, men on horseback and men on foot
    jabbing and stabbing it to a frenzy,
Then the calm heroic matador, elegantly arrayed, gives the
    final thrust, and the crowd shouts bravo bravo, their
    bloodlust gratified.
American Negroes pit dog against dog in a fight to the death,
    bet on it, their mouths drooling at the sight of ripped
    flesh and the frightful sound of the stranglehold.
Cannibals cook and eat Catholic and Protestant missionaries
    without considering their souls, the fatter the better.
What does the perpetual nuclear explosion of the sun care
    about the anthropocentric attitude?
Fission and fusion, reciprocal output and input of energy,
    migmatitization, regeneration, there is soul in more
    things than man.

COMPULSORY IDEOLOGIES

Torquemada the Great Inquisitor said to his victims Believe
    in a merciful God or I will put you to the wrack.
Which he did, pulled bodies apart with stretcher chains,
    crushed their breath out with heavy and heavier weights
    on their chests.
He tortured Jews, Moors, infidels, blasphemists, tortured
    them till they screamed for mercy, tortured them till
    they died.
He was a Dominican prior sanctioned by the Church.
    Thoughout Church territory priests, cardinals, popes,
    kings, queens sanctioned the beheading or burning-at-
    the-stake of dissidents.
Communists cut off the hands of the princess pianist Vera
    Vanova because she would not submit to their revolu-
    tionary doctrines.
Compulsory belief is the sin of sins, enforcement of an
    ideology always a cruel slaughter, conquest less vicious
    than a crusade.

CREDO QUI ABSURDUM

Believe it because it is impossible, believe it because it is
    absurd.
It is shameful for anyone to be born because it is sinful,
    nevertheless the Son of God was really born, no shame
    to it even though birth is shameful,
And it is wholly credible that the Son of God died, was
    buried, and rose again because it is inappropriate and
    incomprehensible.
And it is absolutely certain that Greek gods copulated with
    mere mortals and produced imbecilic Homeric heroes,
But is is doubtful whether our astronauts really set foot
    on the moon because they would have to fly through
    the Pearly Gates of Heaven to get there.

A RATIONAL RELIGION

Church religion is based on sex, redemption from sex, the
    term original sin meaning sexual sin whereby man fell
    from the grace of God,
But if God created everything, then God created sex, and
    God is guilty of the consequences, no theodicy can
    justify the evils thereof.
Christ the symbol of compassion, healing, and uplift for the
    suffering of humanity is truly divine.
Christ the symbol of salvation from sexual sin by vicarious
    crucifixion is a grotesque irrelevance,
The penances, penalties, punishments, rituals, eucharists, sale
    of indulgences a hideous travesty.
The need is a religion to emancipate the mind, emancipate
    the soul, inspire creativity, an ethic of man unto man,
    man unto nature, the rationality thereof needing an
    ideal.

HOLY LAND

Monument Valley is holy land
Red rock buttes like altars stand
Under the wide blue desert sky
Space enters into the soul and eye
Colors are clear, forms are sheer
God is here.
Worship while standing, worship while kneeling
The feeling of thought and thought of feeling.

ENTELECHY

Artistotle's tautological term entelechy, the inner nature of
anything that determines its development, acorn into the
oak, oak into the acorn, egg into the chicken, chicken
into the egg, but what determines the inner nature?
God's will, Allah's will, Brahma's will? Photosynthetic
fortuity, repetitive fixity, evolution, mutation, acquired
characteristics? Aristotle unquestionably questioned the
term himself.
He was a fact-seeker, one of the world's great minds, he
knew the earth was round by the curve of the moon's
eclipse, he sought the reality behind the shadow of the
senses.
Tentative premises led to tentative conclusions, every subject
must have a predicate to be a thought, music is thought
around a set theme, poetry likewise, life a testimony to
its striving nature.

MUTABILITY

The quest is for permanence, change is inevitable,
Accretions, deletions, extinctions variable.
Moment to moment mutable moods
Seek certitudes,
Self stays self despite time's traces,
Constancy no death erases,
Moment to moment an essence clings
To the change that happens to the thought of things.

IMMORTALITY

Eviscerated Egyptian mummies, brains sucked out, guts
    crammed in canopic jars, bodies embalmed, covered
    with gold casts, encased in coffins encased in tombs
Could not preserve the spirits of dead pharaohs. Grave
    robbers and archaeologists scattered the appurtenances
    for immortality along with the treasure trove.
Hindu transmigration of soul, reincarnation in a different
    person, different animal, some kind of different self is
    self-contradictory,
Just another verbal bluff totally lacking actual stuff.
One's concept of integrity is immortal enough.

UNITY

Unity with what? Buddha's eightfold path of righteousness
    ended in the concept of Nirvana,
Cessation of desire, cessation of everything, unity with
    allness, unity with nothingness.
Every stilted concept of unity ends in vacuity, it pervades all
    religions, all ideologies.
Discard your selfish identity for socialized nonentity, join the
    heavenly choir in angelic attire, be one of the multiple
    masses free from caste and classes,
But desire your desirelessness quite ostentatiously, sit on
    your rump steatopygously, contemplate virtue very
    narcisstically.
Bosh bunk and baloney! Get up on your feet and hoe a row
    of pinto beans on a hot summer day, dig potatoes with
    bare hands, shuck corn with callused fingers!
Unity is with the earth and sky.

INFINITUDE OF FRACTIONS

Lacking in concept of zero, Plato was baffled by the concept
of the infinitude of fractions.
It nullified the concept of entity, each fraction of an entity
nullifies the entity fractionated
And the infinitude of fractions nullifies the concept of
infinity.
We proceed by judgement of distinctions, zero is relative to
exchange, a dollar spent on a dollar's worth.

RAINBOW OBSIDIAN

In a chunk of pink-brown rhyolite
A streak of rainbow obsidian shone
Spectrum in stone.
Life is the incarnation of light
Photosynthetic to the bottom of the sea.

A cloudburst ripped ravines down the mountains to the plains,
Flooded arroyos and sagebursh flats,
Cleared except for a drizzle where
Two rainbows blazed in the ozone air
And under the lower arc was hung
A veil of violet mist that clung
On the sage and the hills and mountains and sky.
Deify
Glory be to God in the highest, sing!
Glory to every big and little lovely thing!

And the ugly things, what then of those?
Components of light no less than a rose,
Components of light no less than we
Forever seeking sublimity.

And the girl born blind, what then of her?
Living in a glitter of darkness like black obsidian.
She hears our words, our sounds give sight,
Verbal visualization,
The names of shapes confirmed by touch
The names of colors a subtler sensation
A fantasy world without day or night

Only the light
Of kindness in her blindness.
Consciousness itself is a verbal reflection
Vivid moments interlock
Like the rainbow in rock, rainbow obsidian
Beyond oblivion.

THE STRONGHOLD

Life is a struggle, ideals are the stronghold, a man isn't a man
    unless he's a moral man.
The precept is a pivot for immense freedom around its
    stability, it renders a verbality philosophy utilitarian.
Ideals are the stronghold and if they are false or if they fail,
    the conceit a deceit, the struggle of life is harder.
Cite the douglas fir a curious analogy. It is not a fir, it is a
    spruce, its cones hang down like spruce cones, don't line
    up on a limb like fir cones,
The scientific name Pseudotsuga taxifolia meaning false
    hemlock with comb-like leaves is a verbal fallacy since it
    is neither false nor a hemlock,
It is a real spruce, the strongest construction lumber tree in
    America, and its leaves are pliant to the touch, not rigid
    stiff like the teeth of a comb.
Indian dancers hold fronds in their hands as symbols of ever-
    lastingness beating time with the drumbeat the symbol
    of the heartbeat, stronghold for survival.

DAWN PHOEBE

From his perch under the eaves he greeted the dawn
Phee-eer phee-eer, see here see here
It's time for the morning star to appear,
And it came and a long light silvered on
The rim of the mountains, spread below,
Increased and increased till the sage was aglow
And the phoebe zipped and dipped and nipped
Invisible insects out of the air,
Lit on a pinetip, resting there,
Bending it down like a rocking chair
Saying phee-eer phee-eer phee-eer
I invoked the dawn and it came quite clear,
I woke the world and the world is mine
Including your eaves and the tip of the pine.

MEADOWLARK

His song as bright as his yellow breast
He sings and sings with unquenchable zest,
A series of songs, quite a repertoire
Easy to imitate and he answers with more,
Never a sad note nor a minor third,
A joyous exuberant delightful bird,
Song after song within him spurting springing
So ecstatic he soars up singing awinging.
Wherever he is heard he is welcome, he belongs
Cheering dismal days with lovely shining songs.

BREWER SPARROW

A drab little bird scuttling through the sage,
But when he sings he improvises versatile melodies
    interspersed with surprisingly sweet trills, often marred
    with buzz notes.
Most birds have set songs, the brewer sparrow innovates
    long continuous fascinating phrases.
One evening one flew to our windowsill,
Gave one loud sweet thrilling trill,
All the music of the universe was in it.

PASQUE FLOWER

Grey-blue in green-grey grass
Anemone of the forest fringes
April, May
So soft you dare not walk there roughly
Trampling the fresh spring day
Crushing the consonance of color
Grey-blue, green-grey.

MARIPOSA LILY

Lily of fragility
Butterfly wings aren't so delicate as its lavender-white petals
It grows in aspen groves and lower slopes
Beckons amid the coarse weeds and strangling roots
Whispers why it lives there in the woods.

CASIMIR

He shinnied thirty feet up a eucalyptus to attach a pullrope,
    lopped off branches that might topple the tree the
    wrong way,
Swung himself in the branches recklessly, shinnied down, a
    niche on the leeward, few strokes on the windward, and
    the pullrope felled the tree on exact line.
We sawed and split it up for firewood, soft when green,
    hard as oak when dry, eighteen dollars a cord, over a
    hundred recently.
Casimir. The best worker I ever had, full of zest, tireless,
    effusive, irrepressible. He climbed Mt. Whitney up and
    down on a Christmas Day, quite a jaunt, quite a risk.
He worked several years in an assembly plant for the Ford
    Motor Company, never complained of the monotony,
    did his job and that was that.
His one fear was — if he went to war and got killed, the
    Swedish girl he wanted to marry and for whom he was
    building a house might marry again, and the other
    fellow would get his house along with his wife.
He loved trees, he'd throw his arms around the trunk of a
    madrone and hug it, he'd climb a tall pine just to climb
    it, sniff the aroma of redwood leaves.
Against the advice of park rangers he raced down Bright
    Angel Trail in Grand Canyon, got caught in a blizzard
    coming back up, froze to death.

MIKI

Her father and sister were Christian converts, she kept her
 Japanese sensitivity apart from religion, her drawings as
 symmetrically perfect as a porcelain vase, her paintings
 chunky impressionistic but balanced.
She was in love with a student at the art school, he was of a
 samurai family, his paintings a hybrid of modernistic
 styles, she improved them for him, exhibited them for
 him, helped him gain prestige.
He married her best friend, the blow demeaned her, she
 cooked and housecleaned for a wealthy San Francisco
 family who were kind to her but unappreciative of
 her art.
She sold several paintings, rented a studio, was acclaimed by
 critics, won prizes, her integrity and personal charm
 attracting permanent friendships.
We took her on sketching trips down to the Coast hills, she
 and Gene much alike in their choice of subject-matter,
 often contrary to mine, they preferring modulated
 contours and colors to jagged seacliffs and thundering
 waves.
During the war she married a Santa Fe artist, helped him
 with his work to such a degree he wouldn't let her
 leave him even for a half day to visit us in Taos.
We met her occasionally at the art museum, the same
 sensitive intuitive little Miki, very responsive to the
 New Mexico landscape and Indian atmosphere.
She contributed her own purity to it, her end sudden but
 comforted with the concern of her friends, her husband
 as lavishly attentive to her as she had been to him,
 her Santa Fe doctor a godfather to all his patients.

THE SURGEON

He was a distance runner in high school and college, half
    mile, mile, two mile, he won every race, Midwest
    champion, hero to many a trackfan youngster.
We never equalled his records, nor could we compete with
    the pace he set in his studies, he took time out to be a
    fellow teacher to us.
He got his M.D. and surgery training at Johns Hopkins, came
    back to Missouri, married his childhood sweetheart, rose
    in reputation chief surgeon at the hospital.
She was the right wife for a doctor, neat, pretty, efficient,
    fluffy brown hair, twinkly brown eyes, game for indoor
    or outdoor adventure, canoed with him on the
    Meramec, hiked in the Ozarks, his favorite recreations.
They had three children, two girls and a boy, each self-
    occupied, and she was side-occupied, literary, she wrote
    book reviews for the Post-Dispatch, a volume of poems
    of her own.
He was primarily a gastro-intestinal surgeon, the stomach
    the center of human ills, he advanced hysterectomy
    techniques, endocrine excisions, diverticulitis,
Brain surgery his specialty, tumors, pituitary strangulation,
    cerebral complexities, he had the meticulous tenacity for
    long strenuous operations, he was a distance runner.
His diagnoses were almost infallible, his therapies had a high
    average of success, he was known for his reliability, and
    with the test of years for his consecration and constancy.

THE GENERAL

He was a cavalry captain when my sister married him at the
    border patrol post at Hachita, New Mexico. They walked
    under an archway of crossed sabers to a bower of yucca
    blossoms where the chaplain stood.
He was liked by his troopers, brusque, burly, considerate, his
    big voice shouting orders hearable at the end of a
    galloping line of horses.
Seeing the world war coming he transferred to the Air Force,
    mastered aeronautics, rose in rank major, colonel,
    brigadier.
Commander of the Antilles, cooperating with the Navy to
    prevent German submarines from entering the
    Caribbean he was slated for higher rank but was
    knocked out by a lung hemorrhage.
He retired to Berkeley, retained his cavalry voice to boss
    his relatives and friends, so we called him The General
    whether five-star or one. We defied him on art,
    literature, politics, not on aeronautics or geology.
His father had been chief geologist for the United States,
    had taken him on oilfield charting trips in Oklahoma,
    Texas, Mexico, Alaska, had given him what he punned
    a well-grounded education, he knew what he knew.
Mt. Hayes in Alaska was named after his father, the Brooks
    range named after a cousin, his maternal uncle was a
    geologic mapmaker, it was in his blood, he could make
    hay or Hayes out of any professor.
The red cliff country of New Mexico and Colorado
    fascinated him, the Mesozoic Era, the Morrison
    Formation, dinosaur bones, uranium deposits, nuclear

power for a New Era, formation on top of formation
distinctly marked.
He had no fear of the ghastliness of a nuclear war, he
said he'd rather be blown up and cremated by an
atom bomb in one swoop than have a bayonet
twisted in his guts.
As a General he generalized on military subjects, peace
depends on the maintenance of retaliatory force,
stay strong or get licked,
And he agreed with the retaliation that the basic source
of strength is an exemplary code of conduct, an
exemplary way of living.
His religion was a mixture of commandments.

DINOSAUR BONES AND GIZZARD STONES

They ruled for over a hundred million years, nothing left but
    agatized or opalized bones and acid-polished gizzard
    stones.
Chickens peck pebbles to grind the goop in their craws,
    featherless human bipeds use liquified magnesium
    sulphate crystals as laxatives for the goop in their guts.
They *eat* chickens, they eat cows, pigs, sheep, deer, elk,
    buffalo, fish, oysters, snails, tons of herbage, fruit,
    cereal, they have enormous omnivorous appetites, and
    they are the rulers of the world today.
They fight each other as ferocious as tyrannosaurs, war war
    war, their leaders imbued with ideologies and lust for
    power, Alexander the Great, Julius Caesar the Great,
    Augustus Greater, Napoleon the Great, Lenin the Great,
    Hitler the Great, rah rah rah for conquest.
The friendly little lizard looking up at us from the desert
    dust is a miniature relic of Mesozoic monsters, we may
    be reduced to miniature stature and status ourselves in
    a hundred million years or so,
Tiny computers in our tiny brains as we scuttle back and
    forth after tiny objectives, occasionally swallowing tiny
    grains of sand to abet our tiny grains of sense.

LEMMINGS AND GROUND SQUIRRELS

The lemmings of Norway multiply so excessively they
    commit suicide drowning in the sea.
The ground squirrels of California multiply faster than the
    wild oats they live on, they turn cannibal and eat
    each other.
Masses multiply into crasses, fecundity into redundity, war,
    infanticide, anthropophagy, devastation, havoc.
Whatever the holocaust, love is never lost.

.

BIRTHRIGHT

Think first of the unborn child, health is its birthright, health
and the chance to enjoy the beauty and bounty of the
earth.
Proliferation is a disease, space, grace, love of the land are a
requisite of the soul.
How the city-born child responds to an open field, a cow
grazing in a pasture, a dog running to greet him, the
sight of a bluebird, cardinal, canary, the song of a
songbird!
The Malthusian doctrine was merely economic, population
exceeds production. A eugenic creed will soon supersede
the instinct to breed and breed.
Chastity, prudential restraint, vulgar devices are futile
without a coordinate principle.

LUCRETIUS

Democritus the atom progenitor, Lucretius the atom poet,
   the atom the fundamental unit of existence, building
   block of the universe,
Chemical atoms in molecular compounds, split atoms in
   radioactive explosions, verbal hypotheses progenerating
   actualities.
Lucretius applied the verbalities further than Epicurus, Latin
   a direct linear language like a hurling javelin.
Mallock paraphrased Lucretius further and rounder,
   implications in the English language like atom isotopes
   subtler, profounder.
Lucretius freed fate from the capricious manipulations of
   Greek and Roman gods, none of us can free man from
   the fissions and fusions of fate.

CYCLOTRON

Lawrence was the associate atom smasher, Ernest Orlando
    Lawrence, his cyclotron at Berkeley portending greater
    things than the atom bomb.
I met him but once, my familiarity with the country around
    the joint laboratory at Los Alamos an introduction and
    conversation card.
His knowledge of nuclear physics was far beyond my grasp,
    even the elementary acceleration principles, my
    knowledge of the cliffdwellings and geology in the Los
    Alamos area avidly within his grasp and he pumped me.
He knew the biggest crater in the world was there, eighteen
    miles in diameter, a mountain blew its top, and he was
    aware an accidental atomic explosion might blow a
    bigger crater.
The bomb had been relegated to other physicists, his
    research was for constructive rather than destructive
    potentialities, but he was also aware of the ideological
    conspiracy among some of his colleagues.
From our house on the ridge north of the Berkeley campus
    we saw the midnight flare when the hydrogen lab
    burned down and we suspected sabotage. So did
    Lawrence.
He quietly forestalled a plot that would have given our
    enemies a hydrogen bomb advantage over our secret
    arsenal.
His patriotism was discreet, he didn't flaunt it, he was a
    genial, cultured, broad-minded, very likeable man, a
    great man, his work had powerful implications to
    wonder about.

ODE TO THE BASIC THINKERS

Earth, air, and water were basic enough till they added fire
   and forged fact with fancy beset by fictive gods.
Had they added wheels to the spinning axle of the aeolipile
   they would have run over the gods and propelled the
   facts a little faster.
Nevertheless the Greeks were the first inquirers, first
   founders of basic principles, they had heliocentric
   thinkers a thousand years before Copernicus.
Pythagoras founded the musical scale, ratio of tensional
   vibrational intervals, anticipating Newton's inverse ratio
   of mass attracting mass, particle particle, and he
   projected it to a moral mathematics, celestial
   numerology.
Democritus founded the basic atom, Aristotle the basic
   syllogism, Newton the basic law holding the stars in
   heaven, holding the earth to the stars,
His Principia, written in succinct Latin, a world-shaking
   world-making masterpiece, yet he theologically tried to
   fit a unitary god to his unitary principle, and an alchemy
   to explain the transformations of unitary matter.
Darwin's Origin of Species and theory of evolution provided
   a new basis for biological thinking, but he couldn't
   recognize a benign divine design behind it, no kind-
   hearted deity,
The struggle for survival was brutal, cruel, merciless, no god
   interceded to save the mouse from the cat, the cat from
   the wolf, the wolf from man, man from disaster.
Faraday had the clearest brain, he factualized electro-
   magnetic forces, and the Faraday cage anticipated

81

Einstein's relativity, frame of reference within frame
of reference.
Edison went on from Faraday to invent the electric bulb
and phonograph, the basic instruments for the further
and further development of modern civilization.
The voice of Jenny Lind, the violin of Paganini will never
be heard by present or future generations, the voices of
our virtuoso singers today, the wizard violin of Jascha
Heifetz will be heard for centuries,
And the combination of sight and sound, motion pictures,
television will connect age with age, acquainting peoples
with peoples, perhaps alleviating animosities.
There have been thinkers among all peoples of all times,
unknown thinkers have contributed basic clues for
others, but the mystery of life will remain regardless
of disclosures.
Compassion exists, godliness exists immanent in man himself
extending mercy to the creatures of the earth, our
solace is sharing and contributing what we can.

TIMSY

She strayed to our door a starving pup,
We gave her milk, she lapped it up,
Adopted us then and there.

A mongrel shepherd small and slimsy,
Very affectionate, we named her Timsy,
She went with us everywhere,

Climbed the highest peak in Taos,
Attended discussions in our Berkeley house,
Took the most comfortable chair.

Trips in the desert, trips in the snow,
She danced and pranced and let us know
The things we could really share.

She lived with us happy for thirteen years,
Expressive eyes, intelligent ears,
Eager, alert, aware.

And when she died we layed her on her bed,
Put her in a casket, she didn't look dead,
Her dear little doggy head looked as if she slept.
We wept.

PSYCHIC SONG

Love of life, of man for woman, woman for man, of mother
    for child, love of the creatures of the earth, of special
    places, special possessions is a song in the heart
    pervading the quest for knowledge.
The song one of our Indian friends sang for us one evening
    in our adobe house at Mahualukímo was not of the love
    but of the meaning of life, I recall it to reappraise it.
Sitting by the fireplace beating a drum between his knees he
    finished a series of tribal songs, his voice vigorous,
    virile, vibrant, put his drum aside, stood back in a dark
    corner of the room.
"Now," he said, "I sing ole ole song ole ole mans he taught
    me long ago. I no see him aroun no more. He go away
    somewhere. I sing his song for you."
Strange intervals, half tones, sliding tones, not a chant, no
    beat to it, an undulant fluency, key words with
    implications sliding down from them like the sliding
    tones.
We felt the significance but couldn't interpret it. How our
    Indian friend had memorized those intricate subtle
    sounds was beyond our own ability to retain.
He muted his vigorous voice, transported us back beyond
    our familiar comprehensions and beliefs to a contact
    with unknown psychic sources.

WINDROCK

It stands in the desert strong and solid,
An igneous upthrust over eroded sedimentaries,
A monument to space towering into time,
Rock of ages set secure.
Wind-blown sand will erode it too,
Heat and cold, expansion and contraction,
Crevice it and crumble it level with the land,
And lichen eats the strongest stone.
The ancient Indians carved their petroglyphs
On black basalt with sharp chalcedony scrapers,
Sun symbol, corn symbol, snake lightning, cryptics,
Durable designs drawn on durable rock.
Postulate the words eternity, infinity,
Neither exists.
Inscribe permanent values termporarily timeless,
Rock of reference standing steadfast in the desert
Above the shimmering silver sand
Against the weathering lash of wind
Sustaining the soul.

SACROSANCT PIANO

Dwight Meredith made a shrine of his wife's piano room
    when she died of relapsing rheumatic fever.
He was owner of a wholesale hardware company in St.
    Louis, civic leader, supporter of Washington University,
    helpful to individuals as well as the community at large.
She was a concert pianist, Lucille Meredith, her touch
    sensitive, interpretive, profound, far excelling Paderewski
    or Rubinstein.
He kept her room just as she had left it, except the lid
    over the keyboard and prop lid over the silent strings
    of the Knabe grand were sealed shut.
No other hands than hers should ever play her piano, it was
    sacrosanct, and his four sons respected his sentiment
    knowing it was not an ostentation of grief but a
    consecration for their mother.
It kept her presence alive in the big house, inspired them
    with their own work, all four successful though none of
    them inherited her talent.
Rafe the oldest became a surgeon, Vic an architect, Don a
    sculptor, Jim the youngest a throwback to his grand-
    father Old Hank Meredith known as the farmer-
    philosopher of Hartwell.
He was my age, Jim, we shared viewpoints, we loved to hear
    his mother play, but not until later retrospect did I
    realize what a superlative pianist she was.
A fond conscientious mother she put motherhood into her
    music, everything she played she nurtured for its special
    character, special worth. And her own character seemed
    flawless.

Nice features, low smooth serene concentrative brow, clear
     hazel eyes, straight decisive exquisite nose, shy indrawn
     smile that wasn't shy, beautiful supple hands.
The piano was the instrument of instruments for her, never
     to be used as a percussion instrument thumping out jazz
     depravities or modernistic skitters like chopsticks played
     with stiff fingers.
She gave concerts in St. Louis and Midwest cities, free
     performances in her hometown of Hartwell, a suburb of
     St. Louis, and was revered by everyone who knew her.
When Dwight Meredith died and was buried beside her in
     the Hartwell cemetery, their four sons cremated the
     sacrosanct piano in the back yard, buried the ashes and
     tangled metal in a deep trench at the foot of the two
     graves.

CRITIQUE OF TECHNIQUE

Iambic pentameter, tetrameter, trimeter, anapest,
Long loose lines in a cadence of the caesura,
Pools of rhyme in the stream of sensuous thought,
Wrenched rhymes, print patterns, what technique
    for what subject?
It intertwines in music, implicit significance,
Sermons in tones, sermons in poems.
Shakespeare was his own Polonius
Moralizing in every line he wrote,
Shelley his own Prometheus
Pinnacled dim in the intense inane.
Say yay, say nay, is it right or is it wrong
For the meaning of the song?

THE SCYTHERS

As a boy in New Hampshire the memory for me
Of scythers scything the tall timothy
Is vividly nostalgic, neighbor farmers, three
Mowing the field in staggered tandem rows
Faster than machinery could, strong rhythmic blows,
Smooth shining swaths from which fresh fragrance flows.
They stop in the shade at the end of the glade,
Whet their scythes blade to match blade,
Mow their way back to the stone barricade.
Sweaty but steady they work all day,
And next day they rake the sun-dried hay
With wood-toothed rakes, let no strand stay,
Pitchfork it up on the high wagon mound
Thatching it together so it won't slip around
And tumble the whole load thick on the ground.
They unload it in the barn, don't quit till the supper bell,
Wash up and eat and listen to what their wives have to tell,
Read a book by lamplight, go to bed, sleep well.
I see their furrowed faces, I see their strong hard backs,
And one gave me a smaller scythe to make my own
　　little stacks
Cutting along the edges, slow but improving whacks.
He gave me a silver dollar when I cut a lot one day
And showed me how to swing the scythe to earn
　　a grown man's pay.

NARROWGAUGE LOOP OF THE HIGH COUNTRY

Chug north over Lizard Head Pass to Telluride, over the
Dallas Divide to Montrose, east up the Black Canyon of
the Gunnison to Marshall Pass, south over Poncho Pass
down the Rio Grande valley to Antonito,
Then west over Cumbres Pass back to the starting point on
el Rio del las Animas Perdidas, river of the Lost Souls,
river of found souls for those of us who love the
Rocky Mountains.
All of it high country, wild country, sublime country, deep
canyons, torrential rivers, snow peaks fourteen thousand
feet elevation and up, lush forests, lush flowers,
bursts of exhilaration.
It took terrific work to lay the narrowgauge rails over the
passes and along the base of cliffs, build trestles over
abysses, blast through trememdous dikes of dirt and rock.
Sturdy little engines and sturdy little cars hauled enormous
cargoes, cattle, sheep, pinto beans, winter wheat, coal,
lumber, gold and silver concentrate, uranium ore,
merchandise of all sorts.
Prospectors, miners, geologists, anthropologists, travelling
salesmen, entrepreneurs got on, got off the trains at
stations and hand halts, stockmen, sightseers, women
inured to the lust of men.
There were connections with standardgauge trains, spurs
every direction, the chili line down to Santa Fe a
trespass, rival factions fighting for right of way.
From the 1880's to the 1930's the economy of the high
country depended on the doughty little narrowgauge
railroads, droll stories about them, each train freighted

99

with glamorous pipedreams and practical purposes,
  dramatic conflicts, comic and tragic portents.
The rails were torn up in 1951, end of an epic alas alas,
  'tis sad to see the remnant excursion trains on remnant
  scenic routes.

AVALANCHE

On the cliff-ledged road from Ouray to Silverton thousands
of tons of snow hang overhead during the winter season,
a gust of wind or toot of an auto horn can trigger an
avalanche down across the road into the canyon.
A Congregational minister and his two daughters were swept
to death when he stoppped to put on his tire chains at
the foot of a notorious avalanche ravine.
He was on his way from Silverton to preach at the
Congregational church in Ridgway, perhaps
subconciously trusting the Lord would protect him
from harm.
We saw a crew of men retrieving the body of one of the
girls frozen in the ice after the top snow melted in
March.
A brief Ice Age occured in the Rockies around 500 B.C.,
glaciers polished and scarred the basalt on Grand Mesa
while volcanoes erupted in the Mojave desert.
If the earth wobbles off orbit due to the overweight
and isostatic imbalance of superfluous skyscrapers in
superfluous cities,
Another Ice Age may begin at any minute, sweep the sky-
scrapers in a glacial moraine down to a different axis,
avalanches scoop Los Angeles and its suburb San
Francisco into the sea.
Whither goest thou, little chipmunk, gathering crested
wheat and pine nuts in thy pouches for winter
hibernation in eternity?

BRISTLECONE PINE

The oldest living thing, the bristlecone pine
Older than the redwoods or gods supposed divine.
Three thousand years ere Christ was born
    the bristlecone pine stood high
Atop a barren mountain peak communing with the sky,
Two thousand years thereafter the same tree stood in place
Looking down on the antics of the frantic human race.
In fertile soil it grows in groves near the timberline
Amid the spruce and fir and breakless limber pine.
The nebulae of heaven antedate the bristlecone
With vortex after vortex but nothing there is grown.
Time's inconsequential, grow just to grow
In sun or rain or snow.

ASPEN GOLD

Lift thine heart to the aspen gold
Purpling the blue sky over it there,
Listen to the leaves tinkling in the wind
Twinkle spinned,
Breathe the golden autumn air
Feel the richness of the world unfold.

TAOS ELEGY

Coming out of the Rio Grande gorge onto the vast sagebrush
plateau the first sight of the great Taos Mountain lifting
into the clear blue sky
Gripped us, held us, inspired us forevermore, and 'twas said
on leaving Taos that if we looked back at the Mountain
for a last sight we would come back to it, and we did.
Glorious livable country in those days, the cleanswept sage
valley set in the crescent curve of lower mountains and
foothills like a huge elevated amphitheater for dazzling
sunsets and tingling dawns, white clouds and storm
clouds.
It drew the Indians there, they built their pueblo at the base
of the Mountain synchronized with its shape, the scent
of cedar and piñón firewood pervading it and other
settlements along the streams.
Waterouzels sang on the boulders in the streams, vesper
sparrows in the sage, vireos, warblers, linnets, kinglets
in the cottonwoods and orchards, meadowlarks in the
fields.
Fringed gentians, blue columbine, calypso grew in the vale
where the ski lodge now obtrudes, corn and wheat on
the farmland, apple and peach trees, people were
friendly.
Spanish-speaking, English-speaking, Tiwa-speaking people
were one big Taos family, the derivation of the word
obscure,
Tuata, Tuatao, Tuataos variously pronounced means dwelling
place, Dtao-po means Dancing Water, Dtao-ae Dancing
Leaf.

A blaze of electric lights obliterates the stars now, Taos
   becoming just another suburb of Los Angeles, Chicago,
   New York suffocating the dawn.
Heeleewawa is the Indian word for gone.

FATHOMS OF THE FATHOMLESS

Fathoms of the fathomless, delve no deeper than desire
Motive force of fame, fortune, knowledge, truth.
Seek, aspire.
Isness is isness, the flower flowers,
Fulfills its form and color, its intrinisic powers,
Its desire, forsoothe.

Origin behind origin, below, above, beyond,
No single god could rule the gods behind a single star,
Back and back and back and back what magic wand
Creates the things that are?
A trillion trillion stars and gods compose the pantheon
Nor can it be reduced in scope to a chosen mantheon,
Desire goes deep but not so far.

ABOUT THE AUTHOR

Phillips Kloss was born in Webster Groves, Missouri in 1902.
His first acquaintance with New Mexico came in 1916 when
he worked on his brother's ranch. In 1925 he graduated from
the University of California at Berkeley. Two years later
he was back in New Mexico, this time with his wife,
Alice Geneva Glasier (Gene Kloss). In the years that followed,
living both in New Mexico and on the coast of California,
Mr. Kloss established himself nationally as an important poet
and critic. Phillips and Gene Kloss now live and work in
Taos, New Mexico. In addition to this volume, Sunstone
Press has published *Selected Poems, The Great Kiva* and
Gene Kloss Etchings.